—LIFEKEYS—

Discover Who You Are

DISCOVERY WORKBOOK

Jane A.G. Kise

David Stark • Sandra Krebs Hirsh

BETHANY HOUSE
Minneapolis, Minnesota

Published by Bethany House Publishers
11400 Hampshire Avenue South
Bloomington, Minnesota 55438

Bethany House Publishers is a division of
Baker Publishing Group, Grand Rapids, Michigan.

Printed in the United States of America

ISBN-13: 978-0-7642-0076-2
ISBN-10: 0-7642-0076-3

LifeKey 1

God has an important part for you—yes, YOU!—to play.

LifeKeys grew out of our efforts to help members of our church find meaning and purpose through discovering and affirming:

What they do best
(life gifts and spiritual gifts)

The places or atmospheres that give them the most energy
(personality type and values)

The purposes God placed in their hearts
(passions).

These truths about who you are, why you're here, and what you do best can help you find personal pathways to fulfilling work, activities, and opportunities for service.

This *Discovery Workbook* reflects a desire expressed by our readers and seminar attendees for a personal and concise way of capturing their *LifeKeys*. We suggest that you date this booklet and place it where you can refer to it often to renew your commitments to live the life for which God designed you. For we believe:

• **That each human being is created in the image of God** (Genesis 1:26-27).
We hope that through the *LifeKeys* process, you will come to appreciate the significance of the fact that somewhere inside you is *the image of God,* particularly if you view yourself or your gifts and talents as insignificant.

• **That you were created with a unique, specially chosen blend of gifts** (Psalm 139:13-16).
God gave you everything you need—the truly right gifts chosen just for you. If you struggle to understand how those gifts blend or how they might be used, we hope that through the *LifeKeys* process you might discover the purposes or settings that will clarify the merit of your gifts.

• **God has in mind specific good works for you to accomplish** (Ephesians 2:10).
If you have yet to be a part of the ventures that God has in mind for you, a rich experience awaits you. However, you need to discover that niche—the niche that God promises us is there.

Join us in the process of *LifeKeys* and allow yourself to uncover your gifts, personality, values, and passions—the person that God meant you to be. Place before yourself the wonderful truth that somewhere deep inside of you is a person designed by God. There can be no path more fulfilling than the one that uses your unique gifts as God intended.

LifeKey 2

Doing what comes naturally is part of God's plan.

Proverbs 22:6 tells us: "Train children in the right way, and when old, they will not stray" (NRSV).

The Amplified Bible characterizes "right way" as *in keeping with an individual gift or bent*. There is a right way each of us should go, a natural bent, and it is different for everyone. While many of us are in careers or situations that utilize our life gifts well, some of us are in positions that are a poor fit, either because of uninformed choices, expediency, or the wishes of others.

Let's take a fresh look at the things you do that energize you, where your life gifts lie—that natural bent. For more than seventy-five years, many people have found answers through theoretical work on career choices, particularly that of John Holland. The theory postulates that people's interests can be categorized into six areas of preference—that is, six areas where people tend to cluster as they look for fulfillment through using their life gifts. Holland labeled these six areas as Realistic [R], Investigative [I], Artistic [A], Social [S], Enterprising [E], and Conventional [C]. People who have similar interests or life gifts tend to enjoy similar work, co-workers, and work environments. Their life gifts often derive from these interests. Doesn't that make sense—that we gravitate toward work that we like and do well? These interest areas, then, can help us find our life gifts.

Holland pictured the relationships among these areas by diagramming them as a hexagon:

In Holland's hexagon, typically Realistics have more in common with Investigatives and Conventionals (which neighbor Realistics on the hexagon) than they do with Socials (which are farthest away on the hexagon and have the most dissimilar interests).

Often people find that their interests, when prioritized, reflect this similarity. Some people feel that just one interest area describes them well. Most people are actually a blend of two and sometimes three of the six areas. Their interest areas lie next to each other on the hexagon model. Sometimes, however, an atypical pattern occurs—that is, when someone has interests in opposite areas such as Realistic and Social. While this pattern is normal, it is less common.

Take some time to explore the descriptions of each area to see which sound like you. These are the "home fields" where you can begin the process of identifying your life gifts. Not everyone has all of the life gifts listed under each area. In addition, someone can have life gifts in areas other than his or her home field. Your interest theme, though, is a great place to start the search for your life gifts.

Beginning with the pages for the areas you chose as your natural bent, answer the questions for those gifts you believe may be your life gifts. Then continue through the interest areas in their order of priority to you. Record your top 8-10 life gifts on pages 20-21.

The Realistic Type

General Description

- **Good at fixing or repairing things**
- **Practical, matter-of-fact**
- **Reliable, steady in a crisis**
- **Modest, adept at avoiding attention**
- **A seeker of physical risks**
- **Outdoorsy, athletic, mechanical, hands-on**

In their spare time, Realistics enjoy the out-of-doors, even if they tackle maintenance tasks just to get out in the fresh air. Many own recreational vehicles, sporting goods, and whatever tools they might need to get a job done.

"Let's roll up our sleeves and get it done!"

Typical volunteer activities include providing transportation, maintenance work, leading outdoor activities, repairing furniture or machinery, helping with event set-up, and other tangible tasks.

Realistic Life Gifts

LIFE GIFTS	How have I used this? Dreamed about using this?	Was it enjoyable? (0=terrible; 10=great)	Was it natural? (0=no; 10=yes)	✔ if life gift
Mechanical aptitude—understand and apply the principles of mechanics/physics				
Operating heavy equipment, driving, piloting—includes construction equipment as well as transportation vehicles				
Manual dexterity—skill and ease at using one's hands or fine tools				
Building mechanical/structural devices—design and/or assemble materials as well as execute repairs				
Physical coordination—use multiple muscle movements to a single end, such as needed in athletics, skilled trades, etc.				
Organizing supplies or implements—identify methods that lead to ease of retrieval and maintenance				
Taking physical risks—attracted to activities or occupations with elements of physical danger				
Emotional stability, reliability—react impersonally to situations and thereby stay on course				

The Investigative Type

General Description:
- **Independent and self-motivated**
- **Original and creative**
- **Scholarly and intellectual**
- **Absorbed by your own interests—work seems like play**
- **Motivated to find out how and why**
- **Curious, rational, introspective, perhaps reserved**

"Let's figure this out!"

In their spare time, Investigatives choose complex activities such as skiing, mountain climbing, spelunking, or sailing, where technology and skill play a major role. If they are interested in computers, they know the ins and outs of new hardware devices and how to optimize system performance. For Investigatives, work and play are one and the same.

Typical volunteer activities include setting strategies, collecting or organizing data, researching background information, using computer skills, producing long-range plans, and other intellectual tasks.

Investigative Life Gifts

LIFE GIFTS	How have I used this? Dreamed about using this?	Was it enjoyable? (0=terrible; 10=great)	Was it natural? (0=no; 10=yes)	✔ if life gift
Inventing—imagine or produce something, especially in technical, scientific, or theoretical realms				
Researching—investigate or experiment to gain knowledge, examine theories, or find new applications of current knowledge				
Conceptualizing—originate and develop abstract ideas or theories				
Working independently—work well without guidance or input from others				
Solving complex problems—find solutions to difficult situations or unique issues, usually through logic, analysis, or knowledge				
Computer aptitude—computer skills or systems and software design and development				
Synthesizing information—organize or combine information from different sources so that it is easily understood				
Theorizing—articulate explanations, find connections, or project future trends				

The Artistic Type

"Let's create!"

General Description:

- **Non-conformist, concerned with self-expression**
- **Unstructured, flexible**
- **Original, free-spirited, creative, or imaginative**
- **Have an aesthetic flair**
- **Motivated by bursts of inspiration**
- **Artistically or musically talented**

In their spare time, Artistics often pursue leisure activities that mirror their life gifts. They especially enjoy listening to, seeing, or appreciating their own artistic gifts, or those of others. Writing, photography, interior design, dance, music, or acting are just a few of the specific life gifts they might pursue.

Typical volunteer activities include sharing drama, musical, or artistic talents; taking part in one-time creative efforts; making decorations; handling graphic design tasks; or publicity. Those with writing, musical, or artistic life gifts *may* struggle with making a living wage using those talents and therefore *might* choose to use them avocationally or in volunteer work.

Artistic Life Gifts

LIFE GIFTS	How have I used this? Dreamed about using this?	Was it enjoyable? (0=terrible; 10=great)	Was it natural? (0=no; 10=yes)	✔ if life gift
Acting—project emotions or character by performing roles, either formally in theater settings or informally				
Writing, reporting, technical writing—communicate clearly through written words, including reports, letters, and publications				
Verbal/linguistics skills—adept at studying or learning languages, using and comprehending spoken words				
Musical expression—compose music or perform musically, with voice, body, or instruments				
Creative problem solving—find novel or unusual solutions to problems or issues, especially in artistic or interpersonal areas				
Sculpting/photography/graphic arts/painting—creative expression through artistic mediums				
Creative design through use of space—work with spatial concepts, as in interior design or architecture				
Creative expression through color—coordinate colors and patterns, as in clothing design, decorating, etc.				

The Social Type

General Description:
- **Friendly and cheerful**
- **Kind and generous**
- **Ready to listen, tactful**
- **Cooperative and supportive**
- **People-oriented**
- **Interested in the well-being of others**

"Let's work on this together!"

In their spare time, many Socials choose to coach, teach, offer hospitality to others, or do volunteer work. Because Socials focus so heavily on the needs of people, which can be draining, they sometimes choose Realistic activities for their leisure time to avoid burnout.

Typical volunteer activities include working with community service organizations, planning social events, child care, leading small groups, and counseling or tutoring.

Social Life Gifts

LIFE GIFTS	How have I used this? Dreamed about using this?	Was it enjoyable? (0=terrible; 10=great)	Was it natural? (0=no; 10=yes)	✔ if life gift
Teaching—instruct, demonstrate, train, or guide others in learning information or concepts				
Listening and facilitating—encourage others to volunteer information and discuss issues, either one-on-one or in groups				
Understanding or counseling others—give appropriate advice and guidance tailored to the needs of others				
Conversing/informing—offer hospitality, talk and listen informally about daily events, issues, or personal concerns				
Being of service—consider and act to aid the welfare of others				
Evaluating people's character—discern the motives and values of other people				
Being empathetic and tactful—aware of the feelings of others, able to adjust one's own behavior and respond accordingly				
Working with others—establish harmonious working relationships based on trust and synergy				

The Enterprising Type

General Description:

- **Natural-born leaders**
- **Optimistic and self-confident**
- **At ease with taking risks**
- **Competitive and ambitious**
- **Influential, perhaps seeking status and possessions to influence others**
- **Persuasive and witty**

In their spare time, Enterprising types may pursue political activities or leadership in community organizations. They enjoy attending important sporting events, traveling to key destinations, and entertaining. Participating in sports like tennis or golf has the added benefit of frequenting prestigious clubs or social organizations where they can network.

Typical volunteer activities include fund-raising, leadership roles, recruiting others, giving speeches, and promoting events or outreaches.

"Let's get going!"

Enterprising Life Gifts

LIFE GIFTS	How have I used this? Dreamed about using this?	Was it enjoyable? (0=terrible; 10=great)	Was it natural? (0=no; 10=yes)	✔ if life gift
Public speaking—communicate clearly and with comfort in front of a live audience				
Selling and persuading—advocate the acceptance by others of products, services, ideas, values, or points of view				
Networking and building coalitions—connect people and resources to enhance personal or organizational effectiveness				
Leading— influence others to work together and direct people's efforts toward common missions or goals				
Managing—plan, organize, delegate, and direct projects and resources to attain goals				
Negotiating—aid others in listening to diverse opinions or demands so as to reach agreement or compromise				
Taking action—respond decisively in emergency or stressful situations				
Being adventurous—take above-average financial and interpersonal risks; entrepreneurship				

The Conventional Type

General Description:

- **Practical, methodical, efficient, and orderly**
- **Responsible and conscientious**
- **Contained and content**
- **Careful with things**
- **At ease and accurate with details**
- **Comfortable with structure and routine**

"Let's be dependable!"

In their spare time, many Conventionals choose to vacation in familiar places such as a family cabin or seaside resort where they can renew old acquaintances and seek rest in customary surroundings. They may enjoy hobbies such as collecting (e.g., stamps, figurines), building detailed models (e.g., railroads, dollhouses), playing structured games, and home repairs or decorating.

Typical volunteer activities include working with established organizations such as churches or the Red Cross, organizing supplies and equipment, performing office tasks, establishing procedures, and accounting or auditing.

Conventional Life Gifts

LIFE GIFTS	How have I used this? Dreamed about using this?	Was it enjoyable? (0=terrible; 10=great)	Was it natural? (0=no; 10=yes)	✔ if life gift
Organizing—arrange records, finances, offices, production lines, homes, etc., in a structured manner				
Appraising/evaluating—accurately estimate the value or significance of investments, antiques, real estate, business opportunities, etc.				
Attending to detail—aware of the small elements that make up the whole, as in printed words, administrative tasks, or the environment				
Managing time, setting priorities—arrange activities and schedules so deadlines, appointments, and goals are consistently met				
Calculating and mathematical skills—adept at working with numbers and figures; add, subtract, multiply, divide				
Systematizing—classify information or things for ease of use				
Persevering—follow-through, thoroughness, and patience when handling responsibilities				
Stewardship—conservative handling of money, data, things, and people				

Working With Your Life Gifts—Writing a Sentence

Discovering your life gifts, a part of you since birth, is an exciting process for many people, but you may be asking, "Where do I go from here?" Use one of the following exercises to link your life gifts into a sentence or series of phrases that will help you remember not only what your life gifts are, but how they often work together.

David's sentence is:
I first interview, investigate, and research in order to synthesize and organize information. I then take the information to teach, train, promote, persuade, speak, or act so that I might be of service to people, especially in terms of interpersonal risk.

Jane's sentence is:
I am drawn to things that need to change and use my life gifts of researching, facilitating, synthesizing, writing, and teaching to creatively solve problems in service to others.

Sandra's sentence is:
Personal and spiritual growth for myself and others motivates me. I listen, facilitate, gather, and synthesize information to create a knowledge base from which I can teach, write, coach, and advocate in order to spark insights for myself and others.

EXERCISE A

1. List your top 8-10 life gifts below (those you gave the highest to for enjoyment and how natural they are for you):

2. When you are at your best, which two or three of these life gifts are you using? In other words, which life gifts are central to who you are?

3. Which gifts are normally used first so that you might use your central life gifts (see David's sentence as an example)?

4. Which gifts are typically used after the others are used?

5. Work with your list of life gifts to construct a statement that links them together into a coherent picture of what you do best. Write your sentence below and record it on pages 20-21, "Putting It All Together."

EXERCISE B

Choose three projects/events/tasks that you willingly took part in and enjoyed. These can be from your personal, work, or volunteer roles. Examples might be a social function or family reunion; projects you became involved with because of your hobbies, such as building with Habitat for Humanity; a one-time service opportunity or ongoing volunteer role; or your favorite task at work. Fill in the chart below.

	Project/event/task 1	Project/event/task 2	Project/event/task 3
Why did you work on the project? What motivated you or what made it seem like an attractive option?	*I worked on this project because...*	*I worked on this project because...*	*I worked on this project because...*
What **life gifts** did you use?	*I used:*	*I used:*	*I used:*
What were the **results or products**? Because of your involvement, did things go more smoothly? Were people influenced? Was an event more fun or meaningful? Did you ward off problems or discover new approaches, etc.?	*Because of my involvement...*	*Because of my involvement...*	*Because of my involvement...*
Try to **distinguish** between those life gifts you used to prepare for the result or product and those you used during "the moment"—the results, event, or product	*Life gifts used first:* *Life gifts used during event or product:*	*Life gifts used first:* *Life gifts used during event or product:*	*Life gifts used first:* *Life gifts used during event or product:*

Now look for themes in what you have written. Are there any similarities in your motivations? In what you hope to accomplish? In the gifts you choose to use at different times? Use those themes to construct your own life gifts sentence. Record it on pages 20-21, "Putting It All Together."

LifeKey 3

There are no second fiddles in God's orchestra.

While life gifts are given to all and cover most of the purposes of life—how we relate to other people, find our work, and fill our leisure hours—spiritual gifts allow us to be a part of purposes bigger than what we can do alone. They help us carry out work that God wants to have done.

The *LifeKeys* book contains full descriptions for each of the spiritual gifts as well as suggestions for developing the gifts you discover. As you work to identify your spiritual gifts, please keep the following principles in mind:

- *Spiritual gifts are given to us so we can use them for others.* Each of us receives different gifts so that the body of Christ has what it needs to spread God's message of love. The gifts are given for the common good, not for the benefit of the individual who receives them. We are simply stewards of the gifts we are given.

- *Spiritual gifts are given, not earned.* The gifts we have are in no way a mark of maturity or of how much God loves us. The gifts we have are the ones God wants us to have. Christian maturity is shown not by spiritual gifts, but by the fruit of the Spirit: love, joy, peace, patience, etc. Thus, incredibly gifted Christians can do amazingly stupid things. Instead of putting any gift or person who has a certain gift on a pedestal, look for people who use their gifts wisely and fruitfully, whatever they are.

- *God gave us our gifts for one reason: to put them to use.* If for some reason we choose not to use the gifts God gave us, some part of God's work may be left undone. Therefore, every individual and their unique contributions count.

The inventory below is only part of the process of discovering your gifts. In addition:

- **Instead of completing the following inventory in order, start with the descriptions of spiritual gifts that seem most appealing, likely, or similar to your life gifts.**

- **Read the stories about each gift in *LifeKeys*, chapter 3, or listen to how others have used these gifts. Do these examples sound like things you could do?**

- **Read the statements below for each of the gifts. Check ✔ the statements that apply to you.**

The gifts are grouped into *four categories* that we developed based on the different purposes the gifts seem to serve: *Gifts of the Heart, Gifts of Proclamation, Gifts of Action,* and *Gifts of Inspiration.* While these categories aren't found in the Bible, we find that they help people compare similar spiritual gifts and more easily discover which ones they have. You can go through the inventory page by page, or start with the category that sounds most like you. At the end, you'll give a rating to each gift, as explained on page 18.

HELPS: The ability to work alongside others, attaching spiritual value to the accomplishment of practical, often behind-the-scenes tasks.

☐ I tend to notice and assist with practical tasks that need to be done.

☐ As I do routine tasks, I feel a spiritual link to the ministries or people I serve.

☐ I would rather take on set responsibilities than be involved in leadership.

☐ I prefer to work behind the scenes and often avoid public recognition for what I do.

☐ I receive satisfaction through quietly serving others.

☐ I enjoy working on odd jobs, often seeing a need and tending to it without being asked.

HOSPITALITY: The ability to provide a warm welcome for people that demonstrates God's love by providing food, shelter, or fellowship.

☐ I am comfortable around strangers and care deeply about how they are welcomed.

☐ I enjoy providing a safe environment for those who are in need.

☐ I feel fulfilled when I can open my home to others for food and fellowship.

☐ I can easily concentrate on whether guests feel welcome rather than on whether my house is in order or the food is extraordinary.

☐ I like to create appealing, appropriate environments for people.

☐ I view new relationships as opportunities to pass on God's love.

MERCY: The ability to perceive the suffering of others and comfort and minister effectively with empathy.

☐ I notice when people are hurt, displaced, or rejected and want to reach out to them in their suffering.

☐ I enjoy finding ways to show others how much God loves them.

☐ I can frequently see how to help people who are in need of comforting.

☐ I can easily gain the confidence of those in need.

☐ I tend to see each person as a life that matters to God and reach out to people who are avoided by others.

☐ I enjoy conveying the grace of God to those who feel guilt or shame.

FAITH: The ability to recognize what God wants accomplished as well as to sustain a stalwart belief that God will see it done despite what others perceive as barriers.

☐ I firmly believe God is active in our lives.

☐ Sometimes I sense that God is orchestrating a project or idea. I find it easy to support this when others have doubts.

☐ I believe deeply in the power of prayer and am aware of God's presence in my life.

☐ I am able to believe that God is faithful, even in the face of seemingly insurmountable difficulties.

☐ People often tell me I am an "incurable optimist."

☐ My personal experiences help me believe in the power of faith.

GIVING: The ability to give of material wealth freely and with joy, to further the work of God.

☐ I often give generously and joyfully.

☐ I am resourceful in finding ways to free up my resources to benefit others.

☐ I feel a special connection to the ministries and projects I support financially.

☐ I'd rather give anonymously, for the most part, unless my example might inspire others to be generous.

☐ I tend to manage my own money well, often basing financial decisions on what will be made available for giving.

☐ I feel comfortable and have success with approaching others to give of their resources.

GIFTS OF PROCLAMATION

These gifts involve conveying God's truths or revelations to others.

EVANGELISM: The ability to spread the good news of Jesus Christ in ways that inspire others to learn more about our faith.

☐ I get excited about sharing the Gospel with others.

☐ I enjoy studying questions that challenge Christianity.

☐ I frequently think about people who do not have a faith commitment, wishing they could understand how my faith helps me.

☐ I look for ways that might help others understand the difference Christianity can make in their lives.

☐ I can see how people's needs can be met through faith in Christ.

☐ I can comfortably talk about my Christian faith with others in a way that makes them comfortable as well.

TEACHING: The ability to understand and communicate God's truths to others effectively—in ways that lead to applications in their lives.

☐ I want to make God's truths relevant to life in ways that help people grow and develop.

☐ I like gathering information, especially with the goal of effectively communicating it to others.

☐ I often easily envision how to present spiritual concepts in ways that people find useful.

☐ I love to study the Bible. I receive new insights fairly easily.

☐ When I listen to other teachers, I often think of alternative ways to present the materials.

☐ When I communicate what I have learned, others are motivated to learn more about the Bible and their faith in God.

DISCERNMENT: The ability to recognize what is of God and what is not of God.

☐ I can generally rely on my first impressions of people and whether their motives or character are authentic. I tend to "know" where a person is coming from.

☐ I sometimes sense when something like a book or presentation will bring people closer to God—or cause them to be hurt or pushed away.

☐ In many situations, I find my gut reacting to the circumstance or atmosphere I am experiencing, whether good or bad.

☐ My mind tends to pick up on whether books or speakers are in line with God's truths. Contradictions stand out for me.

☐ I can distinguish sources of energy and motivations in people, whether from the Holy Spirit or others.

☐ I can tell if someone is operating from Jesus' commandment to love one another or if they are putting themselves before God.

KNOWLEDGE: The ability to understand, organize, and effectively use information, from natural sources or the Holy Spirit, for the advancement of God's purposes.

☐ I tend to notice and assist with practical tasks that need to be done.

☐ It is easy for me to gather and analyze information for projects, ministries, or other causes that serve God's purposes.

☐ I enjoy studying the Bible and other books to gain insights and background for God's Word.

☐ I can organize information well to pass on to others.

☐ I seem to understand how God acts in our lives.

☐ At times I find myself knowing information about a situation that has not been told to me by anyone else.

☐ I have insights about how things come together for God's purposes.

PROPHECY: The ability to proclaim God's truths in a way relevant to current situations and to envision how God would will things to change.

☐ I often spot the differences between cultural trends and what we are called to do as people of faith.

☐ I tend to see or think of images that convey God's truth.

☐ To me, repentance, change, and challenge are a healthy part of our spiritual life. I am very aware of the future consequences of choosing one path or another.

☐ When necessary, I am able to confront people with the truth of a situation.

- [ ] It saddens me when others ignore or take lightly life's problems.
- [ ] Often I can interpret God's truths in situations where that truth is encouraging—or even where that truth is unpopular or difficult for listeners to accept.

WISDOM: The ability to understand and apply biblical and spiritual knowledge to complex, paradoxical, or other difficult situations.

- [ ] It is easy for me to make practical applications of the truths found in the Bible, thinking through different courses of action and determining the best one.
- [ ] People often come to me for advice about personal and spiritual matters.
- [ ] I am known for my depth of understanding and insights into complex problems.
- [ ] I am often able to find a profoundly simple solution in the midst of a difficult situation.
- [ ] I have resolved paradoxes by cutting through to the essence of an issue.
- [ ] I help others see God's way in the midst of conflicting viewpoints.

GIFTS OF ACTION
These gifts involve moving individuals or the church toward accomplishing what God wants done.

LEADERSHIP: The ability to motivate, coordinate, and direct the efforts of others in doing God's work.

- [ ] I can motivate others and get people to work together toward a common goal.
- [ ] I have enough confidence in my vision of what could be done to give direction to others.
- [ ] I frequently accept responsibility in group settings where leadership is required.
- [ ] People under my leadership sense that they are headed in a good direction.
- [ ] When necessary, I can make unpopular decisions and work through any conflicts that follow.
- [ ] I can see in advance what people can achieve and know what needs to be done to make it happen.

ADMINISTRATION: The ability to organize information, events, or materials to work efficiently for the body of Christ.

- [ ] I like to organize facts, people, or events.
- [ ] When I am working on a project or effort, it is easy for me to see the necessary steps in the process to solve potential problems.
- [ ] I tend to be frustrated when I see disorganization.
- [ ] I enjoy learning about management issues and how organizations function effectively.
- [ ] I can easily manage schedules, finances, or supplies.
- [ ] I am generally careful and thorough in handling details.

PASTORING/SHEPHERDING: The ability to guide and care for others as they experience spiritual growth.

- [ ] I enjoy encouraging others to develop in their faith.
- [ ] As I work to help others I tend to think in terms of groups, teams, and task forces rather than individual personalities.
- [ ] I can often assess where a person is spiritually; I try to create or look for places where they can connect to enable them to take the next step.
- [ ] I have compassion for those who seem to be getting off track. I long to see them come back to the fold.
- [ ] I would enjoy nurturing and caring for a group of people over a period of time.
- [ ] I like to see people form long-term, in-depth spiritual relationships.

ENCOURAGEMENT/COUNSELING: The ability to effectively listen to people, comforting and assisting them in moving toward psychological and relational wholeness.

- [ ] People tell me that I am a good listener and approach me with dreams and concerns.
- [ ] I often see attributes or gifts in others that they are slow to recognize for themselves.
- [ ] I am usually aware of the emotional state of people around me, whether they are content or whether something is bothering them.
- [ ] In stressful situations, I often find myself able to give perspective on what is positive in a way that others find helpful.

☐ I tend to have more faith in people than they have in themselves.

☐ I sympathize easily with others and am tolerant of their shortcomings, yet I enjoy helping people mature in their faith.

APOSTLESHIP: The ability to minister transculturally, starting new churches or ministries that touch multiple churches.

☐ I am excited about working in multiple church settings and diverse religious communities.

☐ I am interested in how the Gospel can be brought to those who have never heard it.

☐ I am attracted to new ministries, churches, or settings at home or abroad where a whole new approach to evangelism or service is needed.

☐ Presenting the Gospel to a different culture or in a different language sounds fulfilling.

☐ The idea of living in or visiting different places excites me.

☐ I have often envisioned myself as a missionary.

GIFTS OF INSPIRATION

These gifts make us aware of God's power in our lives or provide new energy for the work of God's kingdom.

HEALING: The ability to call on God for the curing of illness and the restoration of health in a supernatural way.

☐ I am naturally drawn to those who are sick either in spirit or in body.

☐ Sometimes God seems to work through me to bring physical, spiritual, relational, or emotional healing to others.

☐ I am aware of God's presence and listen for God's guidance on how to pray in each situation where healing is desired.

☐ Often I can sense whether a person's problems are physical or emotional in origin.

☐ When petitions for healing are spoken, I find myself wanting to pray.

MIRACLES: The ability to call on God to do supernatural acts that glorify God.

☐ I find myself praying for things that are obviously beyond the natural capacity of people.

☐ I seek for God to be glorified however my prayers are answered.

☐ I have witnessed God perform supernatural acts when I have prayed for intervention.

☐ I have seen others accept the Christian faith through these displays of the impossible being accomplished.

☐ I have faith that miracles happen even today.

☐ Often I see God at work when others only see coincidences.

SPEAKING IN TONGUES: The ability to speak in a language, known or unknown to others, supernaturally.

☐ Occasionally I have prayed in words or language(s) I have never before heard.

☐ Sometimes in prayer, my love for God feels so strong that I have difficulty expressing myself in words.

☐ I have been inspired or have inspired others to step out in faith through the use of personal prayer languages.

☐ I find during worship that my tongue wants to express itself in syllables I do not understand.

INTERPRETATION OF TONGUES: The ability to interpret spiritual languages.

☐ I can interpret the words of others who have spoken in languages ("tongues"), even though I have never before heard the languages.

☐ I understand how messages given through the use of tongues serve to glorify God, Jesus, or our faith.

☐ When somebody speaks in tongues, I feel the Holy Spirit giving me the ability to interpret or speak.

Spiritual Gifts Summary

Consider each gift again. Is it something that you've often done? Something that you can envision yourself doing with more training? Something that intrigues you but you haven't had opportunities to explore? Or something that is of no interest to you? Regardless of the number of statements you checked, rate your endowment of each of these spiritual gifts as follows, writing the numbers in the blank in front of each gift:

5. This is definitely one of my spiritual gifts.

4. This is probably one of my spiritual gifts.

3. I am unsure—I need to learn more about this gift or experiment with ways to use this gift to find out if I have it.

2. This is probably not one of my spiritual gifts.

1. This is definitely not one of my spiritual gifts.

Gifts of the Heart

___ Helps

___ Hospitality

___ Mercy

___ Faith

___ Giving

Gifts of Proclamation

___ Evangelism

___ Teaching

___ Discernment

___ Knowledge

___ Prophecy

___ Wisdom

Gifts of Action

___ Leadership

___ Administration

___ Pastoring/ Shepherding

___ Encouragement/ Counseling

___ Apostleship

Gifts of Inspiration

___ Healing

___ Miracles

___ Speaking in Tongues

___ Interpretation of Tongues

Choose your top five spiritual gifts and record them on the "Putting It All Together" chart on pages 20-21.

LifeKey 4

If you know yourself, you can find your God-given place.

Each of us have natural preferences for four key processes—how we are energized, how we take in information, how we make decisions, and how we approach life. Taken together, these preferences add up to your personality type—your essential nature.

To clarify this concept of preferences, try signing your name below with your *non-preferred* hand:

For most people, this feels unnatural, awkward, difficult, or time-consuming. Now write your name with your *preferred* hand.

Most people say that this feels natural, easy, and comfortable. These concepts apply to our psychological preferences as well— while we can learn to use any of the eight preferences, we *prefer* using the ones that are most natural to us.

To help you understand your unique and innate personality, we use a theoretical construct based on Jungian psychology and popularized through the Myers-Briggs Type Indicator® tool (MBTI®). Jung saw personality type as a tool through which we can better understand ourselves and therefore deepen our spiritual side.

While the following exercise can help you identify your personality type, you may wish to use the MBTI® tool, which is a questionnaire designed to help you sort your preferences. Ask your seminar leader, pastor, or local community education program for referral to a qualified MBTI® practitioner, or call the publisher of the MBTI® tool, Consulting Psychologists Press, at 800-624-1765 (*www.cpp.com*).

(continued on page 22)

My Life Gifts:

1.

2.

3.

4.

5.

6.

7.

8.

9.

10.

Putting It

My Passions:

As I reflect on my *LifeKeys*, I see my mission as:

My Life Gifts Sentence:

Date:

l Together

My Top Eight Values:

1.

2.

3.

4.

5.

6.

7.

8.

In making decisions about where I work or serve, I need to remember:

My Spiritual Gifts:

1.

2.

3.

4.

5.

My Personality Type:

____ ____ ____ ____

Factors that are important to me as I choose places or settings for work or service:

YOUR TYPE PREFERENCES

EXTRAVERSION or INTROVERSION

This preference pairing deals with how you are **energized**—either from the external world [E] or from the internal world [I]. This preference is *not* about how outgoing or shy you are. Check ☑ which statement from each pair describes you best:

Appeal to Extraversion
- ☐ Lots going on, active
- ☐ Interruptions are stimulating, fun
- ☐ Outgoing, communicative atmosphere
- ☐ Group or team approach
- ☐ Discussion for processing ideas
- ☐ Busy, energetic places
- ☐ Thoughts and feelings shared readily
- ☐ Experimentation, then reflection
- ☐ Focus on the outer world
- ☐ Emphasis on people and things

Appeal to Introversion
- ☐ One thing going on, reflective
- ☐ Interruptions are distracting, annoying
- ☐ Reserved, protective atmosphere
- ☐ Solo or partnership approach
- ☐ Introspection for processing ideas
- ☐ Quiet, contemplative places
- ☐ Thoughts and feelings guarded until ready to share
- ☐ Reflection, then experimentation
- ☐ Focus on the inner world
- ☐ Emphasis on thoughts and ideas

Overall, the preference that describes me best is Extraversion (E)___ or Introversion (I)___.

SENSING or INTUITION

This preference pairing deals with how you **gather information**—through your five senses [S] or through hunches, analogies, and connections [N].[1] Check ☑ which statement from each pair describes you best:

Appeal to Sensing
- ☐ Practical, common-sense focus
- ☐ Accuracy required
- ☐ Past experience valued
- ☐ Methodical approaches used
- ☐ Current reality emphasis
- ☐ Rewards for following procedures
- ☐ Improving the real world
- ☐ Practical application of learning is key
- ☐ Command of details, procedures is honored
- ☐ Predictable routines

Appeal to Intuition
- ☐ Innovative, insightful focus
- ☐ Creativity required
- ☐ Inspiration valued
- ☐ Novel approaches used
- ☐ Future possibilities emphasis
- ☐ Rewards for finding a better way
- ☐ Designing the ideal world
- ☐ Theoretical understanding of learning is key
- ☐ Agility making connections and hunches is honored
- ☐ Variety, unpredictability

Overall, the preference that describes me best is Sensing (S)___ or Intuition (N)___.

[1] *The "N" is used for "Intuition" because the "I" has already been used for "Introversion."*

THINKING or FEELING

This preference pairing deals with how you **make decisions**—using objective, logical principles [T], or by stepping into the shoes of those involved [F]. Check ☑ which statement from each pair describes you best:

Appeal to Thinking
- ☐ Emphasis on logic, analysis
- ☐ Ideas for data and things
- ☐ Decisions made fairly but firmly—few exceptions
- ☐ Business first—orientation toward task
- ☐ Recognition desired for meeting or exceeding task requirements
- ☐ Analyze—find the flaw
- ☐ Objective—decisions made with the head
- ☐ Skepticism and controversy enrich productivity
- ☐ Drive for competency
- ☐ Reasons—clear rules and principles

Appeal to Feeling
- ☐ Emphasis on harmony, diplomacy
- ☐ Ideas for people
- ☐ Decisions made empathetically—considering the circumstances
- ☐ Camaraderie first—orientation toward people
- ☐ Praise desired for personal effort as tasks unfold
- ☐ Sympathize—find the positive
- ☐ Subjective—decisions made with the heart
- ☐ Acceptance and sympathy enrich productivity
- ☐ Drive for relationship-building
- ☐ Values—discerning what is important to each person involved

Overall, the preference that describes me best is Thinking (T)___ or Feeling (F)___.

JUDGING or PERCEIVING

This preference pairing deals with how you choose to **approach life**—whether you plan your work and work your plan [J] or take advantage of the moment [P]. Check ☑ which statement from each pair describes you best:

Appeal to Judging
- ☐ Organized and efficient
- ☐ Emphasis on planning projects and events
- ☐ Planning ahead is key to reducing stress
- ☐ Settled and decided
- ☐ Work before play
- ☐ Much is accomplished through regular, steady effort
- ☐ Focus on tasks and timetables
- ☐ Stated goals and outcomes
- ☐ Emphasis on coming to closure on decisions
- ☐ Enjoy finishing tasks

Appeal to Perceiving
- ☐ Flexible, allowing for multiple tasks
- ☐ Emphasis on allowing projects and events to unfold
- ☐ Allowing for contingencies is key to reducing stress
- ☐ Open to late-breaking information
- ☐ Work and play coexist
- ☐ Much is accomplished through last-minute effort
- ☐ Focus on processes and options
- ☐ Stated general parameters
- ☐ Emphasis on gathering new information before deciding
- ☐ Enjoy starting tasks

Overall, the preference that describes me best is Judging (J)___ or Perceiving (P)___.

Now record below the preferences that describe you best:

_____	_____	_____	_____
E or I	S or N	T or F	J or P

Through class discussion or as you read your type description (*LifeKeys*, pages 148-163), record your observations below:

• What factors are important to me as I choose places or settings to work or serve? What will help me be as effective and satisfied as possible?

• In what ways, if any, does my current setting conflict with or enhance my natural style? Where am I and my setting the same/different?

• What actions can I take to change my current setting or my attitude toward it?

• How can I honor my type and the person I am? How can I select future settings that work best for me?

As you discover ways in which your personality type might influence the places or atmospheres you choose to work or serve in, record your observations on pages 20-21, "Putting It All Together."

THE SIXTEEN TYPES AT A GLANCE:
Contributions to Workplace or Spiritual Community

ISTJ	ISFJ	INFJ	INTJ
• Being dutiful and responsible conservers of tradition • Having hardworking, dependable, and pragmatic habits • Using past experience effectively • Bringing order and logic to what they do	• Providing stability, improving efficiency • Offering sensible and matter-of-fact attention to daily concerns of people • Adding a sense of dignity and respect to the community • Honoring commitments; others can rely on them	• Understanding the feelings and motivations of others • Finding creative ways for people to accomplish and enjoy tasks • Lending future-oriented ideas to planning and development • Offering insights about how individuals and systems interrelate	• Envisioning systems or adjusting strategies to create a better world • Breaking new ground, shifting paradigms, and changing the way people think • Synthesizing diverse information and viewpoints • Pushing others toward their goals
ISTP	**ISFP**	**INFP**	**INTP**
• Finding expeditious ways to handle a project, dispensing with red tape • Grasping reality to troubleshoot and solve problems • Setting an example of authenticity, pointing out hypocrisy • Sharing a storehouse of facts and details when asked about their special interests	• Providing caring, gentle, behind-the-scenes help • Meeting individual needs personally and genuinely • Giving immediate, direct help to people • Sharing concrete, practical, and precise information when asked	• Bringing a compassionate, caring, and personal focus • Reminding others of their values and the worthiness of striving to meet them • Providing a positive vision for the future • Enriching others with creative ideas	• Searching relentlessly for universal truths • Determining the long-term consequences of any given plan or strategy for action • Providing clear, analytical frameworks for understanding • Contributing intellectual insights
ESTP	**ESFP**	**ENFP**	**ENTP**
• Paying attention to what needs doing/fixing right now • Meeting practical needs in the most efficient way • Reminding others of the joys of this life, at this present time • Solving problems in a straightforward, logical manner	• Reminding others how to appreciate each other and all they have • Being generous with time and talents • Communicating warmth, excitement, and acceptance • Keeping track of many things at once	• Initiating and promoting ideas to help others grow • Adding vision, warmth, and enthusiasm to community undertakings • Connecting resources, especially people and ideas • Sparking a sense of excitement and adventure	• Initiating new projects, direction, etc. with enthusiasm and energy • Providing insight and imagination to tasks and projects • Exhibiting resourcefulness in dire or complicated situations • Debating, asking the tough questions
ESTJ	**ESFJ**	**ENFJ**	**ENTJ**
• Organizing to meet day-to-day concerns • Demonstrating consistent habits based on principles • Insisting that "hard questions" be answered and acted upon • Following through to see that tasks are done correctly, results are seen	• Preserving traditions from one generation to the next • Making people feel welcome and valued—gracious and giving to others • Knowing what matters for people and organizations • Handling tasks efficiently, promptly, and accurately	• Monitoring values and integrity • Supporting others with warmth and encouragement • Believing in the positive nature of people • Articulating messages that others want or need to hear	• Developing long-range plans for people and organizations • Understanding how parts relate to the whole • Bringing a logical order to problems • Offering intellectual and philosophical insights

Preferred Settings for Work or Service

ISTJ

- Quiet atmosphere that allows for privacy
- Goals met at a steady pace
- Experienced, committed co-workers
- Expectations known: clear, well-documented procedures
- Stable assignments and responsibilities

ISFJ

- Secure, predictable, organized setting
- Caring, responsible, courteous co-workers
- Stable, enduring organizations where the emphasis is on serving others, not competitiveness
- Roles and responsibilities are clear
- Calm, quiet, private atmosphere

INFJ

- Meaningful, service-oriented vision
- Considerate, harmonious co-workers who share similar values
- Rewards for individual integrity, creativity, and insights
- Private space for quiet and reflection
- Opportunities for individualized approaches

INTJ

- Decisive, intellectually challenging, effective co-workers who take a long-range view of issues
- Room for creativity, independence, and autonomy
- Emphasis on problem-solving, outside-the-box thinking
- Private space for reflection
- Willingness to implement ground-breaking ideas

ISTP

- Minimal rules and requirements, emphasis on autonomy
- Little red tape or roadblocks to efficiency
- Hands-off, egalitarian norms
- Action-oriented co-workers, focused on immediate problems
- Logic and principles are upheld

ISFP

- Organizations that contribute to community and/or individual well-being
- Adaptable, flexible, and accepting setting
- Empathetic, cooperative, supportive, harmony-seeking co-workers
- Quiet, private, aesthetically appealing atmosphere
- Emphasis on practical tasks

INFP

- Values, as inspiration and motivation, are upheld and acted out
- Service to a larger, common purpose
- Artistic spaces for quiet and reflection
- Friendly, committed, values-oriented co-workers
- Flexibility and creativity emphasized over routine and structure

INTP

- Emphasis on using systems and models to rationally solve complex problems
- Rewards for self-direction, creativity
- Scholarly, competent co-workers
- Maximum flexibility, minimal policies and procedures
- Private spaces and time for thought

ESTP

- Goals are clear yet flexibility exists in how they are met
- Lively, results-oriented co-workers who believe that work and fun can coexist
- Casual, non-bureaucratic organization
- Emphasis on tangible facts, logical processes
- Latest, best resources available to accomplish work efficiently

ESFP

- Spontaneous yet stable and secure workplace
- Energetic, easygoing co-workers
- Clear roles and responsibilities but room to carry them out with flair or style
- Collaborative, team orientation
- Lively, interactive, colorful surroundings

ENFP

- Stimulating, forward-looking creative team environment
- Flexible, imaginative co-workers focused on possibilities
- A variety of people, tasks, and perspectives
- New, challenging pursuits brainstormed and launched
- Room for spontaneity, friendship, flair

ENTP

- Flexible, change-oriented, entrepreneurial efforts or organizations
- Highly competent, effective, competitive co-workers
- Strategic, big-picture focus
- Freedom to act or change
- Rewards for risk-taking and innovation

ESTJ

- Place for everyone/everything and everything in its place
- Past, relevant experience is honored
- Hierarchical structure based on logic of function, order
- Stable, efficient, and predictable
- With hardworking, task-oriented co-workers who plan times for fun

ESFJ

- Stable, efficient settings that value loyalty, teamwork, and sensitivity
- Practical systems and structures oriented toward people as well as goals
- Conscientious, cooperative, friendly co-workers
- Facts and values are both considered
- Decisiveness is honored

ENFJ

- Community or social service orientation with strong ideals
- Sociable co-workers who focus on the common good
- Harmonious, supportive, creative environment
- Clear, results-oriented organizations that respond to people's needs
- Room for personal growth, self-expression

ENTJ

- Focus on pressing issues or problems, with rewards for meeting them
- Large-scale projects, challenges, or organizations
- Efficient structures and people in alignment with master plan
- Dedicated, tough-minded, confident, competent co-workers
- Logical, orderly, analytical

LifeKey 5

Seek the values that strike the right chord with God.

What do you value? Think of the things that
- feel important to you
- define your fundamental character
- supply meaning to your life and work
- influence the decisions you make
- compel you to take a stand
- describe atmospheres where you can be productive.

You may not know what you value until an event, circumstance, or person comes into direct conflict with that value—or until you purposefully try to identify what is important to you.

There are three ways to complete this values clarification exercise: The book *LifeKeys* includes a set of fifty-one values cards that you can sort and prioritize. You can make your own set using 3 x 5 cards. Or, you can number the values listed on this page.

VALUES CLARIFICATION EXERCISE

Using the prompt "As I make important decisions, this is how I value _____," rate each of the values listed below as:

1. This is very important to me.
   Limit yourself to eight values rated very important to you!

2. This is important to me.

3. This is not very important to me.

___ Accuracy
___ Achievement
___ Advancement
___ Adventure
___ Aesthetics
___ Artistic Expression
___ Authenticity
___ Balance
___ Challenge
___ Competency
___ Competition
___ Conformity
___ Contribution
___ Control
___ Cooperation
___ Creativity
___ Efficiency
___ Fairness
___ Family
___ Financial Security
___ Flexibility
___ Friendship
___ Generosity
___ Happiness
___ Humor
___ Independence
___ Influence
___ Integrity

___ Learning
___ Leisure
___ Location
___ Love
___ Loyalty
___ Nature
___ Organization
___ Peace
___ Perseverance
___ Personal Development
___ Physical Fitness and Health
___ Power
___ Prestige
___ Recognition
___ Religious Beliefs
___ Responsibility
___ Security
___ Self-Respect
___ Service
___ Stability
___ Tolerance
___ Tradition
___ Variety
___ _____
___ _____
___ _____

Working With Your Values

Record your eight most important values:

Value	My definition
1.	
2.	
3.	
4.	
5.	
6.	
7.	
8.	

What are your thoughts about the values you selected? Are there any surprises?

GENERAL VALUES APPLICATIONS

Listed below are several questions to help you work with your values. Read through all of the questions. You need not work through every question. Instead, choose those that are most appropriate for your current situation.

1. **To evaluate your current work/service environment:** List again your eight top values. Then review the list on page 26 one more time to choose the eight values you believe are most important in your work/service environment. Are there any conflicts between the two lists? (Comparing lists of values can also be useful for husband/wife discussions or team building.)

Do values explain any conflicts or tensions you feel about your current work/service environment? How might this be resolved? You may need to talk through alternatives with someone you trust.

2. **To consider whether a job or service opportunity fits your values or what setting is needed to harmonize with your values:** Assume that you have found a job or service opportunity that fits with your life gifts, spiritual gifts, personality type, and passions. What is the atmosphere needed for it to honor your top eight values?

MY NEXT SEASON OF LIFE

As you think about the next season of your life and how your values might change: Define the "next season" of your life: new job, empty nest, end of school, retirement, whatever you believe your next stage will be. How do you think your values might change? Re-sort the values to find the top eight values for the next season of your life.

My "next season" of life will be _____.		
My current top values	My "next season" top values	My definition of this value
1.		
2.		
3.		
4.		
5.		
6.		
7.		
8.		

1. What in your life may be difficult to control as your values change?

2. What areas of change will be stressful for you? Are there any potential conflicts? What are two or three concrete steps you can take to move toward your "next season" values?

3. How does this values clarification change your priorities of God, family, work, and friends? How can you maintain balance?

MORE VALUES EXERCISES

Use these questions to further clarify your values.

1. From your outward actions, what might other people—a friend, co-worker, family member—discern as your top values? Are there conflicts in how you view yourself versus how they perceive your actions?

2. Consider whether any of your top eight values are in conflict with each other. For example, valuing financial independence and generosity can be problematic, as can valuing adventure and stability.

3. Pull out your calendar and think about the past week. Write out your week's activities to see how they correspond to your top eight values. Consider if any goals need to be set to bring your lifestyle more in line with your values.

LifeKey 6

You are called to serve where you can harmonize with God's song in your heart!

Passions are desires or purposes that bring us joy. *Webster's* defines passion as a powerful emotion: "fervor, ardor, enthusiasm, zeal." The word *enthusiasm* comes from the Greek phrase *en theos,* "with God." Thus, if you are *enthusiastically* pursuing a passion that God has put in your heart, you are doing it *with God!*

People often begin to discern their passions through one of four approaches. Which approach sounds most like you?

___ **The "One Talent" approach**—do you look for chances to use a *specific* life gift or spiritual gift in a variety of arenas?

___ **The "Make Me an Offer" approach**—are there certain leaders or ministries with visions or missions that appeal to you? Are there roles to fill within those efforts that fit with your gifts?

___ **The "Right Under Your Nose" approach**—if you broaden your definition of passions, might yours appear right where you are, in the settings you enter regularly?

___ **The "Dreamer" approach**—do you find it easy and exciting to simply dream about what you might do for God in order to discover where to focus your efforts?

Below are questions for each approach. Start with the approach that is most like you.

FOR THE "ONE TALENT" PEOPLE

1. The following list is meant to trigger your own thoughts. It is by no means exhaustive nor all-inclusive—seriously try to think of *other* areas. Which skills might you enjoy using?

☐ Artistic expressions	☐ Foreign languages	☐ Photography	☐ Time management
☐ Car repairs	☐ Gardening	☐ Political pursuits	☐ Travel
☐ Carpentry	☐ General management	☐ Reading	☐ Word processing
☐ Coaching athletics	☐ Graphic arts	☐ Research	☐ _____
☐ Computers	☐ Home repairs	☐ Sewing	☐ _____
☐ Cooking	☐ Mathematics	☐ Social justice issues	☐ _____
☐ Crafts	☐ Office administration	☐ Speaking	
☐ Driving	☐ Organizing	☐ Storytelling	
☐ Financial planning/budgets	events/parties	☐ Teaching	

2. Look back through prior experiences, your life gifts, and your spiritual gifts. Which are the most enjoyable for you to use? How could you put those gifts to use more regularly?

FOR THE "MAKE ME AN OFFER" PEOPLE

1. In the space below, write down the passions or interests of people you know who are already *en theos*. How could you help them accomplish their dreams? (Remember, sometimes the project may not be as important to you as the character of the person in charge.)

2. Find out what ministries and missions your church actively supports. Which of these are of interest to you?

3. Get a listing of the most recent volunteer opportunities available at your church or at another organization that seems appealing to you. Some churches have notebooks or databases with descriptions of available opportunities. Take time to review it for ideas. Write down which tasks interest you.

4. Contact the formal or informal leadership of your spiritual community in areas that seem attractive to you (for example, adult education, outreach, member involvement, music, etc.). Ask about their volunteer needs.

FOR THE "RIGHT UNDER YOUR NOSE" PEOPLE

1. Which of these groups do you most easily relate to, wish you could help, or feel drawn to because of personal experience or frequent encounters?

Age group:

- ☐ Children
- ☐ Teens
- ☐ College/young adults
- ☐ Singles
- ☐ Young marrieds
- ☐ Parents of young children
- ☐ Parents of teens
- ☐ People approaching mid-life
- ☐ Empty nesters
- ☐ Seniors

People with practical needs:

- ☐ Education (or tutoring)
- ☐ Finance/budget issues
- ☐ Nursing/health care assistance
- ☐ Housing needs
- ☐ Immigration issues
- ☐ Legal advice/concerns
- ☐ Maintenance or repair needs
- ☐ Parenting concerns
- ☐ Prayer ministries
- ☐ Workplace issues

People with counseling needs:

- ☐ Substance abuse
- ☐ Families experiencing relationship problems
- ☐ Grief support
- ☐ Marital counseling
- ☐ Mental health issues
- ☐ Parents of special-needs children
- ☐ Spiritual direction/discipleship
- ☐ Support groups
- ☐ Terminal illnesses
- ☐ Transition counseling

Ministries to specific populations:

- ☐ Business and professional men or women
- ☐ Community/neighbors
- ☐ People with disabilities or illnesses
- ☐ Ethnic groups
- ☐ Refugees
- ☐ International students
- ☐ Missionaries
- ☐ New church members
- ☐ Unemployed
- ☐ The disenfranchised

Others:

2. List below the roles you play or have played during the past three years. Examples are employer, employee, parent, child, teacher, neighbor, citizen, patient, counselor, customer. What concerns arose for you in those roles? Which ones could you act upon?

FOR THE "DREAMERS"

1. If you had no fear of failure and limitless time and resources at your disposal, what would you do (after your trip around the world!)? What are some of the longings of your heart that you would finally be able to address? What "dreams" continually cross your mind?

2. Name three people who have accomplished something that you would like to do or who have had a tremendous positive impact on your life. Because of them, toward what causes or purposes might you like to turn your efforts?

Name of person	What they did	What I might do
1.		
2.		
3.		

3. If you could do some of the things either you *should* do or you have *wanted* to do for a long time, what would these be?

LifeKey 7

Keep in step with God's syncopation for YOUR life.

What do each of the five biblical principles for making life choices mean to you? Take a moment to rank the five principles in your own life, giving a "1" to the area you feel you manage best and a "5" to the area where you believe you could most improve. Where are you in control? What are your strengths? What don't you have time for? Record any insights for making better life choices.

My
Ranking   Biblical Principle

_____   **1. Put first things first—seek the kingdom of God.**
Do you successfully find time to pursue your own spiritual practices? If this is a struggle for you, check your personality type description (pages 148-163 of *LifeKeys*) for Possible Spiritual Helps that might be appealing to you.

_____   **2. Know your mission.**
If you do not yet have a mission statement, construct one using the information from "Putting It All Together" (pages 20-21) and the process outlined on pages 251-253 of *LifeKeys*.

_____   **3. Know your limits.**
Are you often scattered or exhausted? Make a list of the activities that *re-create* you or bring you rest—hobbies, sports, relationships, solitude, time in nature, etc. Do you find time for these? Remember that you may need to purposefully schedule your time for re-creation to avoid being drained by the urgent needs of each day.

_____   **4. Simplify—aim for balance in your life.**
Are you in control of your possessions and commitments or do they control you? Are there any that keep you from things you consider truly important? Do any take too much of your time in view of other priorities?

_____   **5. Reflect on people who seem to have enough time.**
If finding time to act on your passions seems impossible, consider how others manage to have enough time to act with God. Identify one step that you could commit to now, or plan for two or three *months* from now what would enable you to begin to fulfill the passions you identified through *LifeKeys*.

LifeKey 8

Fulfillment is making music where God wants you to play.

True servants can perform the most *insignificant* tasks—not because they are worth little but because they understand their own worth in God's eyes. Jesus served from a place of power, not weakness. He stands ready to help you serve in the same way.

Philippians 2:4 reminds us, "Each of you should look not only to your own interests, but also to the interests of others." To serve from a place of fullness, we need to look to our own interests, yet we still need to look outward as well. Contemplate your life. Are you finding balance between meeting your needs and those of others? If not, what are some steps you could take?

CONSIDER THE SIX PRINCIPLES OF BIBLICAL SERVANTHOOD.
How do these principles mesh with your views on service? Journal or discuss each one. Which seem true? Which seem difficult to act on? How do these redefine or expand your definition of the word *servant*?

• Serve from a place of fullness, not emptiness.

• Biblical servants ensure that their own needs are met so they can focus on the needs of others.

• Finding ways to use our giftedness for God requires conscious commitment. God leaves the choice of serving or not serving in our hands.

• As we open our hearts to God's purposes, we become available to move to the places God wants us to be.

• Following God's leading does not always result in the world's approval. What will result is your own fulfillment as an instrument of God.

• The right place to serve is where God calls you to serve, whether far away or right where you are.

Your next step...

What is your next step? *LifeKeys* is an individual journey. Very few people complete such a journey in a few days, weeks, or even months; the progress varies greatly depending on where a person starts. As you finish these pages, you may be just at the beginning of your personal discovery.

Can you say with your heart, in a paraphrase of Ephesians 2:10, "For I am fearfully and wonderfully made by God, created in Christ Jesus for good works, which God prepared in advance for me to be my way of life"?

It is true—you are a valuable soul just as you are! Whatever God has chosen for your good works, they are chosen to fit your way of life, your calling, your mission. May your *LifeKeys* help you find true fulfillment!

We encourage you to make a commitment to continuing the process. Below are suggestions that others have found helpful:

1. On your own, with a friend, or with a small group, work through the book *LifeKeys,* using the discussion questions at the end of each chapter.

2. Either alone or with a small group, choose another way to continue the *LifeKeys* process. Other groups have:

   • **spent time in deep discussion over life gifts and spiritual gifts, helping one another discern which gifts they have;**

• **chosen a service opportunity for which they could volunteer together;**

• **read a follow-up book together. Favorites of other groups include:**

   • *Finding and Following God's Will* (Jane Kise, Minneapolis: Bethany House Publishers, 2005). An in-depth look, through stories and biblical teaching, at how God guides us.

   • *SoulTypes: Matching Your Personality and Spiritual Path* (Sandra Hirsh and Jane Kise, Minneapolis: Augsburg Fortress Publishing, 2006). Understanding how your personality type influences your spiritual practices.

   • *Working With Purpose* (Jane Kise and David Stark, Minneapolis: Augsburg Fortress Publishing, 2004). The five "corporate callings" we have as Christians and ways to influence corporations, without apologizing or proselytizing, to carry them out.

   • *The Path* (Laurie Beth Jones, New York: Hyperion Books, 1996). A guide to writing personal mission statements.

   • *The Life You've Always Wanted* (John Ortberg, Grand Rapids, Mich.: Zondervan, 1997). Understanding and working toward God's vision for our lives.

   • *What's Your Type of Career?* (Donna Dunning, Mountain View, Calif.: Davies-Black Publishing, 2001) or *Do What You Are*

(Paul Tieger and Barbara Barron-Tieger, New York: Little Brown, 1995). Both provide career direction, using your personality type.

- *Looking at Type and Spirituality* (Sandra Hirsh and Jane Kise, Gainesville, Fla.: Center for Applications of Psychological Type, 1997). A deeper look at the impact of personality type on one's spiritual practices.
- *LifeTypes* (Sandra Hirsh and Jean Kummerow, New York: Warner Books, 1989). Gives a life view of a person's personality type over the years.

3. Work through the exercises for one of the specific *LifeKeys* applications: Volunteer and Service Opportunities (p. 255), First Career Direction (p. 263), Midlife Transitions (p. 269), and Retirement Planning (p. 277).

4. If you identified growing closer to God as your first priority, consider meeting with a minister or spiritual director for suggestions on prayer and study that might help you.

5. Meet with a volunteer coordinator or people involved with specific ministries to understand how you might join with them.

THOUGHTS I'D LIKE TO REMEMBER

Action Steps I'd Like to Take

BOOKS I MIGHT READ...

PEOPLE I MIGHT MEET WITH...

QUESTIONS I NEED ANSWERED...

BIOGRAPHICAL INFORMATION

JANE A. G. KISE, Ed D, is a freelance writer and consultant, specializing in team building and school staff development. She also teaches seminars and speaks across North America on prayer, constructive use of differences, and unlocking our lives for God. She is the author or coauthor of more than a dozen books, including *Finding and Following God's Will; Did You Get What You Prayed For; Working With Purpose;* and *SoulTypes.* Kise is also a frequent contributor to *Guideposts* and other magazines. She holds a BA from Hamline University, an MBA from the University of Minnesota, and a doctorate in educational leadership from the University of St. Thomas. She and her family live in Minneapolis.

DAVID STARK is director of Changing Church Forum, a ministry of Prince of Peace Lutheran Church. He is also vice president of BusinessKeys International. He divides his time among three roles: pastor, business consultant, and trainer, and is coauthor of *LifeKeys* and *LifeDirections,* and author of *Christ-Based Leadership* and his own small group materials, *People Together* and *Growing People Through Small Groups.* Stark holds a BA in biology and an M Div from Princeton Theological Seminary. He and his family reside in Minneapolis.

SANDRA KREBS HIRSH has authored or coauthored more than a dozen books on psychological type, including *SoulTypes* and *LifeTypes,* and *Introduction to Type® in Organizations,* which has sold over two million copies. She is a management/organizational consultant, coaches individuals, writes, and is much in demand worldwide for her expertise in personality type and team building. Hirsh holds a BA from Arcadia University, an MA from the University of Pennsylvania, and a master's degree in human relations from the Carlson School of Management at the University of Minnesota. She lives in Minneapolis.

Information on *LifeKeys* Resources and Web Sites

- *Christ-Based Leadership.* David Stark. Bethany House Publishers, 2005.

- *Find Your Fit Discovery Workbook.* Jane Kise and Kevin Johnson. Bethany House Publishers, 1999.

- *Find Your Fit Leadership Resource.* Jane Kise and Kevin Johnson. Bethany House Publishers, 2000.

- *Find Your Fit: Dare to Act on God's Design for You* (*LifeKeys* for Teens). Jane Kise and Kevin Johnson. Bethany House Publishers, 1998.

- *Finding and Following God's Will.* Jane Kise. Bethany House Publishers, 2005.

- *Growing People Through Small Groups.* David Stark and Betty Veldman Wieland. Bethany House Publishers, 2004.

- *Introduction to Type® and Coaching.* Sandra Hirsh and Jane Kise. CPP, 2000.

- *Introduction to Type® in Organizations.* Sandra Hirsh and Jean Kummerow. CPP, 1998.

- *LifeDirections: Discovering the Gift of God's Guidance.* Jane Kise and David Stark. Bethany House Publishers, 1999.

- *LifeKeys Leadership Resource* (2nd ed.). Jane Kise, David Stark, and Sandra Hirsh. Bethany House Publishers, 2005.

- *LifeKeys: Discover Who You Are* (2nd ed.). Jane Kise, David Stark, and Sandra Hirsh. Bethany House Publishers, 2005.

- *LifeTypes.* Sandra Hirsh and Jean Kummerow. Time Warner Books, 1989.

- *SoulTypes* (2nd ed.). Sandra Hirsh and Jane Kise. Augsburg Fortress Books, 2006.

- *Work It Out!* (2nd ed.). Sandra Hirsh and Jane Kise. Davies-Black Publishing, 2006.

- *Working With Purpose.* Jane Kise and David Stark. Augsburg Fortress Publishers, 2004.

www.lifekeys.com
Check out train-the-trainer schedules and new products.

www.janekise.com
Download a basic leaders' guide for *LifeKeys,* check out speaking engagements, new publications, and share your stories.

www.changingchurch.org
Explore online *LifeKeys* tools and *LifeKeys* training events.